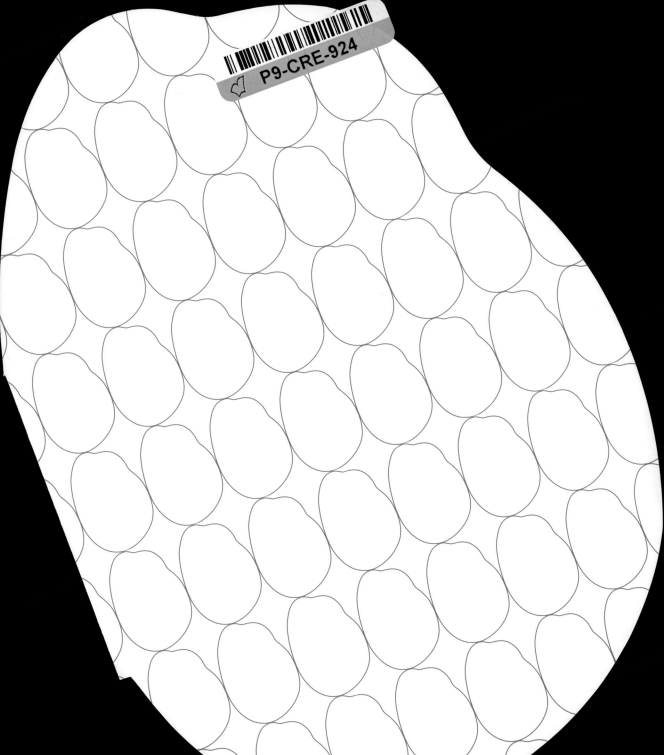

POTATOES

50 Easy Recipes

CREATED BY
ACADEMIA BARILLA

PHOTOGRAPHY BY
ALBERTO ROSSI
CHEF LUCA ZANGA

RECIPES BY
CHEF MARIO GRAZIA

TEXT BY
MARIAGRAZIA VILLA

GRAPHIC DESIGN
MARINELLA DEBERNARDI

EDITORIAL COORDINATION ACADEMIA BARILLA
CHATO MORANDI
ILARIA ROSSI

3

CONTENTS

ONE THOUSAND WAYS TO SAY POTATO

It has a squat appearance, sometimes a bit lumpy, and almost always awkward and clumsy. Its color is yellowish, red, or purple, and yet, the potato is a diamond. Easy to cultivate and maintain, endowed with a particular flavor, and open to every culinary fantasy, it has a thousand faces: all delicious, and highly prized in kitchens around the world.

The ways to prepare the precious tuber are almost unlimited. Potatoes can be served hot or cold, with or without the peel, in pieces or whole, seasoned or plain. They can be boiled in water, roasted in the oven, steamed, cooked in a casserole, pan fried or deep-fried. They can be eaten alone, but also with many other ingredients; they form the canvas for many possible masterpieces.

The Many Personalities of a Tuber

The potato, which exists in thousands of different varieties, is so versatile that it can be a simple and comforting food, as in the classic mashed potatoes or the unassuming boiled version, seasoned with a drizzle of oil and a pinch of salt, but is also so delicious as to become the quintessence of transgression, as in the timeless French fried potatoes. It can be the element that makes the difference in traditional preparations: a focaccia with potatoes is much fluffier; a pizza with potatoes is more tempting; a polenta with potatoes is more delicate ...

This tuber of a thousand resources can even go from start to finish in a menu without losing appeal. It can whet your appetite if served as an appetizer or with an aperitif; constitute the main ingredient of a tasty first course, such as a plate of soft steaming gnocchi; help to create a nutritious main course if matched with meat, fish, cheese, or eggs; or make a pleasant side dish. Lastly, it can be used as an ingredient in the dough for a dessert, to give more fluffiness, or to give character and flavor to a dessert, as with our original potato sorbet.

Nutritional Virtues and Practical Advice

The potato is rich in vitamins and minerals, especially vitamin C and potassium, both in the peel and in the potatoes. Due to its high content of carbohydrates, found mainly in the form of starches, and to its modest number of calories, the potato can replace bread in low-calorie diets, and also prove a valuable ally for people intolerant of the gluten in grains. Each variety is suited to a particular culinary destiny: potatoes with yellow paste, for example, which have a compact pulp, are excellent for frying or salads, while those with white paste, mealier, are ideal for recipes such as gnocchi or croquettes. When boiling potatoes, it is always best to start with cold water and boil them with the skins on (after having carefully washed them!) so the pulp does not take in too much water. When peeling and slicing them raw, it is best to soak them in cold water so they do not darken.

Enjoy the Classic Dishes, Try the New

Academia Barilla, an international center dedicated to the diffusion of Italian gastronomy, has selected 50 recipes using potatoes. Some are typical dishes of the Bel Paese, such as the gattò di patate (potato torte) proper to the cuisines of Campania and Calabria; the trenette with pesto sauce, potatoes and green beans, from the Genoese tradition; or the potato fricos, typical of Friuli. Others were created by combining the charm of this tuber with other ingredients from the tricolor culture of gastronomy: cheeses such as Montasio or Parmigiano-Reggiano, preserved meats such as speck, bacon or cotechino sausage, as well as chestnuts, porcini mushrooms, baccalà. Some recipes, such as the blini, born in Russia, or the rösti, from Switzerland, do not belong to Italian gastronomic history. However Academia Barilla chose them because they follow these principles: respect and love for primary ingredients, simplicity capable of becoming elegance, executive ability, and above all the joy of sharing.

BREAD
FOR THE POOR

In addition to gold and silver, the Spaniards discovered potatoes in Peru. Originating in the Andean region and cultivated by the Indians since prehistoric times, as evidenced by archaeological excavations, potatoes attracted the attention of Spanish conquistadores around the first half of the 16th century.

Traveling Potatoes

We do not know the exact date when potatoes appeared in Europe, and there are many contradictory versions of the story. There are even some who would have it that Christopher Columbus imported them on returning from his 1492 voyage, even though there are no documents confirming this. It is likely, however, that it was the waves of the Atlantic that brought the first potatoes to the Irish coasts following the sinking of several ships of the Spanish fleet returning from Peru in 1565. Ireland, in the grips of hunger, accepted the potato as a blessing. Any prejudices were overcome, and cultivation rapidly became widespread for that root of strange appearance and particular flavor which, owing to its underground development, could survive destruction and looting and stave off starvation.

8

In Europe

Potatoes are documented as having provided food, during the second half of the 16th century, for the garrisons of Philip II in Flanders, spreading throughout the Netherlands and Germany. In 1587, Pope Sixtus V (Felice Peretti, 1520-1590), after receiving a potato as a gift from Spain, aided in its introduction to Belgium. In 1573, potatoes appeared in the Hospital de la Sangre in Seville for the diet of the poor and sick, and in a painting from 1645 by Bartolomé Esteban Murillo, St. James distributes them among the beggars. The Barefoot Carmelites introduced them to Italy, in Genoa, where Padre Nicolò Doria arrived from Spain and founded the first Italian monastery in 1584. In 1667, a case of potatoes was a gift to the grand duke of Tuscany, who had some of them cooked boiled, sliced, breaded, and fried, while the rest were kept aside for cultivation and examination by Francesco Redi (1627-1697), a scientist at the court of the Medici.

The news that began to spread all around the world about potatoes, as well as other exotic tubers and fruits arriving from the Americas, created a great confusion and contributed to mystifying the potentialities of potato. At that time in Europe, the known edible plants were cultivated by means of seeding. Suspicions spread that the potato – whether for its appearance or for its unusual manner of reproducing – had diabolic properties. It was said that this plant grew because the devil wanted to poison the earth with his spittle. The bulbous and irregular tubercles brought to mind something deformed, and popular superstition held the potato to be responsible for many contagious diseases. Toward the end of the 18th century, with the increasing frequency of famines and the need to find alternatives to wheat or corn flour, the governments of various countries embarked upon outright promotional campaigns to encourage cultivation of the potato. In 1651, Frederick William I of Prussia threatened to cut off the nose and ears of anyone who refused to cultivate them. His son, Frederick II, distributed potatoes to farmers for free, obliging them to grow them, and in support of his edict, he had his armed Dragons intervene.

Parmentier, the Prophet of the Potato
In France, the potato was met with obstructionism by doctors, who claimed it was hard to digest, and by agronomists, who claimed that it would ruin the land (in fact, its cultivation requires proper fertilization, a practice that, at the time, was uncommon and poorly defined). In 1771, an award was announced for the substitution of grains in the basic diet. It was won by military pharmacist and agronomist Antoine

Augustin Parmentier (1737–1813), who, during his time as prisoner of the Prussians during the Seven Years' War (1756–1763), became the first Frenchman to witness the virtues of the potato, which Frederick II had forcibly inserted into the rations of troops and prisoners.

A Kiss from the Queen of France for a Potato

At the court of Louis XVI, Parmentier prepared an official dinner in honor of Benjamin Franklin, the American ambassador in Paris, composed exclusively of potatoes cooked in many different ways. To spread their cultivation, Parmentier obtained permission from the king to plant potatoes at the gates of Paris in the sandy soil of Les Sablons, known for being especially sterile and used only for military training and racing horses. Due to the softness of the ground, the potatoes thrived, and Parmentier, probably copying a trick of Frederick II, requested permission to stand a guard of soldiers during the day, to provoke curiosity among the local farmers. At nighttime the soldiers were withdrawn and the potatoes, no longer protected but now considered "valuable" because of the strange maneuvers, were stolen by the curious population, who ate them and planted them. When the field blossomed, Parmentier offered a bunch of the flowers to Queen Marie Antoinette, who rewarded Parmentier with a kiss, while the king affirmed, "One day France will be grateful to you for having found bread for the poor."

The Spread of the Potato

In Italy as well, the cultivation of the potato, relegated until that time to marginal lands, spread through northern Italy after the Napoleonic campaigns. After overcoming mistrust, the potato spread rapidly in certain countries to the point of giving rise to irrational monocultures, which later led to famine. The worst was the one that struck Ireland between 1845 in 1847, when the vast crops of potatoes, which had become nearly exclusive as the economic and nutritional foundation of the Irish, were devastated by the appearance of *Peronospora*, one of the most terrible plant pathogens afflicting this member of the Solanacea family, driving the country to its knees and provoking a large-scale emigration to America.

Numerous documents and publications produced in the late 18th and early 19th centuries magnify the manifold possibilities for using the potato. Christian Friedrich Reuss listed the versatility of the small tuber, from which one could obtain flour, starch, salt, yeast, and even beer, wine, and spirits. Even art found its muse in the potato. Great painters such as Van Gogh, Millet, and Lieberman, and poets like Shakespeare, Goethe, and Grass, celebrated it in their creations.

By this point the potato's battle against prejudice and mistrust could be declared to have been won, and books began offering recipes for how to prepare it in various manners. In addition to the fifth edition of his *Il cuoco galante* (a treatise on gastronomy), in 1801 Vincenzo Corrado produced his *Trattato delle patate* (treatise on potatoes), offering a rich list of preparations: potatoes in polenta, in cream, in croquettes, in fried puffs, roasted, filled with butter. He also outlined the prototype, subject to later adjustments, for *patate in gnocchi* (potato gnocchi).

11

Then it was the Americans who, regaining possession of their legacy, spread the use of potatoes. Sliced very thin and fried in boiling oil – as previously introduced in England in the 1930s – they flooded the planet during the Second World War.

The versatility of the maligned tuber now makes it one of the primary foodstuffs in the human diet, but without that kiss from the queen, it would probably still be looking for a testimonial, and our cuisine would be different. Even today, at the historical Père Lachaise Cemetery in Paris, potatoes blossom every year on the tomb of Parmentier.

Giancarlo Gonizzi
*Curator of the **Academia Barilla Gastronomic Library***

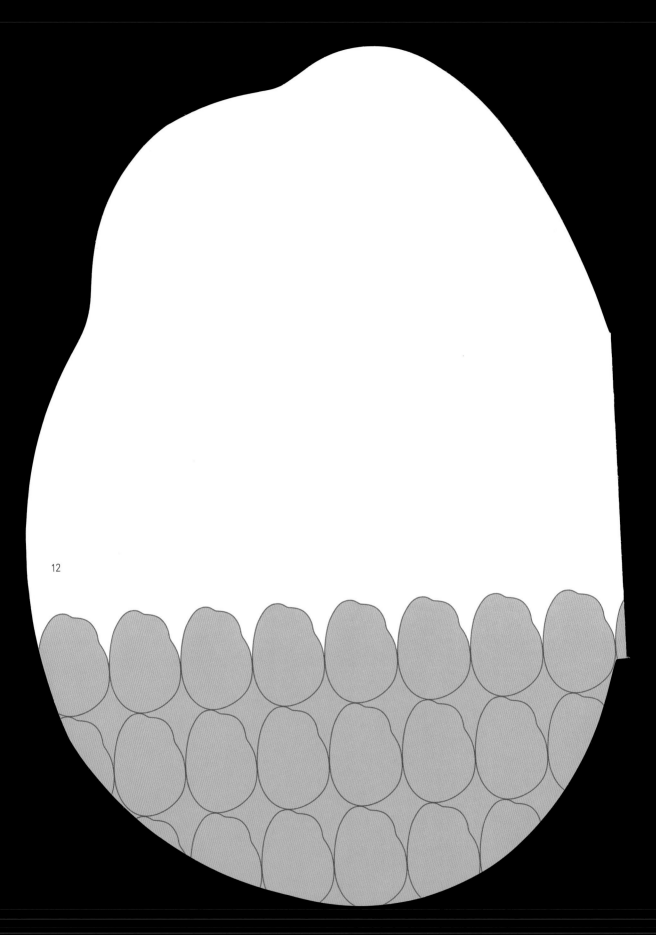

12

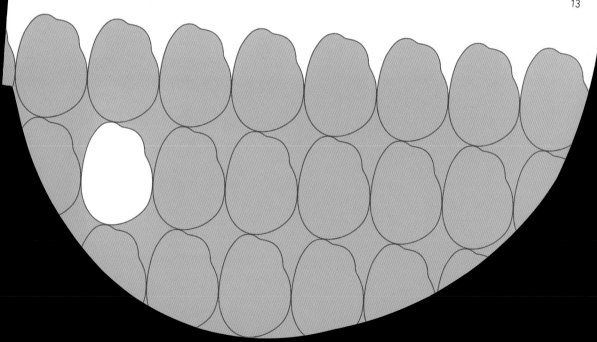

APPETIZERS
AND APERITIFS

POTATO BLINI
WITH TROUT EGGS

INGREDIENTS FOR **4** PEOPLE

200 g (2/5 lb) boiled potatoes
200 ml (3/4 cup + 1 1/2 tbsps) milk
35 g (1/4 cup + 1 tbsp) flour
2 eggs
30 g (1 oz) butter
30 g (1 oz) trout eggs
salt and pepper

METHOD

In a bowl, mix the potatoes, mashed through a potato ricer, with the flour, eggs, and milk. Season with salt and pepper. Work until you obtain a thick batter.
Let it rest for about 30 minutes. Grease an appropriate pan with part of the butter. Prepare each blin by pouring a spoonful of the mixture into the pan.
Cook for a minute, then turn the pancake over, finishing with another minute of cooking.
Repeat until all the batter has been cooked.
The pancakes you will obtain will be about 1 cm (2/5 in) thick, and these will serve as the base for the trout eggs, to be cooked separately in a pan with the remaining butter.

14

Preparation time: 40' Rest: 30'
Cooking time: 2' (for each blin) Difficulty: easy

POTATO FLAN WITH PARMIGIANO-REGGIANO CHEESE

INGREDIENTS FOR **4** PEOPLE

450 g (1 lb) boiled potatoes
200 ml (3/4 cup + 1 1/2 tbsps) cream
3 egg yolks
2 tbsps water
50 g (1 3/4 oz) Parmigiano-Reggiano cheese, grated
35 g (3 1/2 tbsps) cornstarch
20 g (4 1/4 tsps) butter
salt and pepper

METHOD

In a bowl, mix the potatoes, mashed through a potato ricer, with the cream, egg yolks, Parmigiano-Reggiano, and the cornstarch dissolved in 2 tablespoons of water, then season with salt and pepper.
Melt the butter and grease appropriate individual molds. Fill them three-quarters full with the mixture and bake at 170°C (340°F) for about 20 minutes.
Let the flan cool for 5 minutes before removing it from the molds.

Preparation time: 40'
Cooking time: 20' Difficulty: easy

FOCACCIA
WITH POTATOES

INGREDIENTS FOR 4 PEOPLE

For the focaccia
350 g (2 3/4 cups) flour, type "00"
250 ml (1 cup) water
150 g (1/3 lb) boiled potatoes
1 tsp sugar
50 ml (3 1/2 tbsps) extra virgin olive oil
15 g (2 1/2 tsps) yeast
12 g (2 tsps) salt

For the genovese brine
50 ml (3 1/2 tbsps) water
25 ml (1 1/2 tbsps) extra virgin olive oil
7 g (1 tsp) coarse salt

For the garnish
150 g (1/3 lb) potatoes
salt

METHOD

Wash the potatoes and boil them with the skin on. Drain, then mash them with a potato ricer.
Arrange the flour into a well on the pastry board. Gradually add the sugar and the water, into which the yeast has been dissolved. Stir in the mashed potatoes, the oil, and lastly, the salt. Continue to knead until the dough is smooth and elastic. Let the dough rest for about 10 minutes. Form a ball and let rise for 40 minutes on the work surface.
Roll out the dough to a thickness of 1 cm (2/5 in) and place it in a baking pan greased with olive oil. Let stand for another 10 minutes, then use your hands to press it out so that the baking pan is completely covered with dough. Meanwhile, using an appropriate instrument, finely slice a peeled potato, blanch it in salted water for 1 to 2 minutes, then let it cool. Arrange the slices of potato over the focaccia.
Prepare the brine in a bowl by combining the water, extra virgin olive oil, and coarse salt. Emulsify the mixture using a whisk, then sprinkle over the surface of the focaccia.
Let rise in a warm area for 90 minutes. Bake at 250°C (480°F) for about 20 minutes.

Preparation time: 20' Rising: 2 h 30'
Cooking time: 20' Difficulty: medium

POTATO AND
MONTASIO CHEESE FRICOS

INGREDIENTS FOR **4** PEOPLE

200 g (2/5 lb) Montasio cheese
300 g (2/3 lb) potatoes
20 g (1 1/2 tbsps) butter
20 g (3 tsps) salt

METHOD

Wash the potatoes and boil them with the skin on, to the point where they still maintain some of their consistency. Let them cool, then peel, and grate using the large holes of a grater. Then grate the Montasio cheese, or cut it into cubes. Melt the butter in a skillet, brown the potatoes, and season with a pinch of salt. Add the cheese and mix together. Let the potato-cheese mixture brown like a pancake. After about 5 minutes, turn it over to brown the other side, again for 5 minutes.

DID YOU KNOW THAT...

The Frico is a simple and very tasty farm-style appetizer (but also excellent as a main course dish) originating in the mountains of Carnia. One of the typical recipes of the cuisine from Friuli-Venezia Giulia, it is prepared – whether crispy or soft – using the dairy-farming glory of the regional gastronomy: Montasio cheese.

Preparation time: 30'
Cooking time: 10' Difficulty: easy

POTATO FRITTERS

INGREDIENTS FOR 4 PEOPLE

700 g (1 1/2 lbs) potatoes
100 g (3 1/2 oz) Parmigiano-Reggiano cheese
100 ml (1/3 cup + 1 1/2 tbsps) water
50 g (3 1/2 tbsps) butter
60 g (1/2 cup) flour
2 eggs
salt
nutmeg
oil for frying

METHOD

Wash the potatoes and boil them with the skin on in slightly salted water.
After cooking, peel, then mash them into a bowl using a potato ricer.
Add the Parmigiano-Reggiano cheese and some grated nutmeg.
Meanwhile, pour the water into a saucepan. Add the butter cut into cubes,
and a pinch of salt. Bring to a boil.
Pour the flour, previously sifted, into the saucepan all at once. Mix well using
a wooden spatula until the dough comes loose from the walls of the saucepan.
Let cool, then stir in the eggs one at a time.
Combine together the two dough mixtures and correct for salt, if necessary.
Using a pastry bag, form rings of dough on greased baking paper, then let them
slip into the boiling oil.
Fry, drain, and set them to dry on paper towels, then season with salt.
Alternatively, you can form the fritters using two tablespoons, carefully dropping
the dough balls directly into the oil.

22

Preparation time: 40'
Cooking time: 5' Difficulty: medium

FRIED POTATO
AND FISH BALLS

INGREDIENTS FOR **4** PEOPLE

550 g (1 1/5 lbs) cod, about 350 g (3/4 lb) cleaned
280 g (3/5 lb) potatoes
100 g (3 1/2 oz) chopped onion
100 g (3/4 cup + 1 tbsp) flour
150 g (1 1/4 cups) breadcrumbs
3 eggs
extra virgin olive oil
oil for frying
1 bunch parsley
1 bunch chives
salt and pepper

METHOD

Wash the potatoes and boil them with the skin on, in slightly salted water.
After cooking, peel them and mash using a potato ricer.
In the meantime, peel and fillet the cod, removing all the bones.
Trim, wash, and chop the herbs.
In a saucepan, cook the chopped onion over low heat with a drizzle of extra
virgin olive oil. Add the cod, chopped into pieces, and cook over high heat,
breaking the pulp into threads using a wooden spoon. Finish cooking the fish
and place it in a bowl. Add the mashed potatoes and finely chopped parsley and
chives. Season with salt and pepper, and let the mixture cool.
Shape it into balls about the size of walnuts, roll them in the flour, then in the
beaten eggs, and lastly in the breadcrumbs. Repeat the breading process.
Fry in abundant boiling oil. Drain the potato and fish balls and set them to dry
on paper towels, then season with salt.

Preparation time: 45'
Cooking time: 5' Difficulty: medium

POTATO PIE

For the dough
65 g (2 1/3 oz) boiled potatoes
125 g (1 cup) flour
2 egg yolks
18 g (1 1/4 tbsps) butter
6 g (3/4 tsp) yeast
2 g (scant 1/2 tsp) fine salt
10 g (1 1/2 tsp) butter for greasing the pan

For the filling
150 g (1/3 lb) ricotta
20 g (3/4 oz) bacon
20 g (3/4 oz) Gruyere cheese
15 g (1/2 oz) Parmigiano-Reggiano, grated
chopped parsley
salt and pepper

METHOD

In a pastry board, knead the potatoes, mashed through a potato ricer,
with the flour, egg yolks, softened butter, crumbled yeast, and lastly,
the fine salt. Work until you obtain smooth, soft dough.
Separately, mix the ricotta with the salt, pepper, Parmigiano-Reggiano, chopped
parsley, bacon, and Gruyere cheese cut into cubes.
Using a rolling pin, flatten the dough to a thickness of about 5 mm (1/5 in); line a
buttered pie pan with part of the dough. Add the filling and cover with another layer
of dough. Trim off the excess dough and seal the edges, using the tines of a fork.
Prick the surface of the pie with the prongs of a fork to allow the steam
that forms during cooking to escape.
Let the pie rise in a warm place for at least 30 minutes.
Bake at 160°C (320°F) for about 20 minutes.
Let it sit for a few minutes before serving.

Preparation time: 40' Rising: 30'
Cooking time: 20' Difficulty: medium

POTATOES WITH CASTELMAGNO CHEESE AND EGGS

INGREDIENTS FOR 4 PEOPLE

4 medium potatoes
4 eggs
60 g (2 oz) Castelmagno cheese
30 g (1 oz) butter
salt and pepper

METHOD

Peel the potatoes and boil them in slightly salted water for about 15 minutes.
Let cool, then scoop out a portion of the interior lengthwise, leaving a cavity.
Arrange the potatoes on a baking pan lined with parchment paper.
For each potato, break an egg into the interior, then season with salt and pepper
and a dab of butter. Sprinkle crumbled Castelmagno cheese over the potatoes
and bake for 10 minutes at 180°C (350°F).
Serve immediately.

DID YOU KNOW THAT...

The origin of Castelmagno cheese – one of the gastronomic highlights of the
province of Cuneo – dates back to around the year 1000, although the first
historical evidence of a cheese with this name, used by the people as a way
to pay a duty on goods, dates from the 13th century.

Preparation time: 30'
Cooking time: 10' Difficulty: easy

PIZZA WITH BACON AND POTATOES

INGREDIENTS FOR **4 PEOPLE**

For the dough
650 g (5 1/4 cups) flour for pizza
375 ml (1 1/2 cups + 1 tbsp) water
5 g (3/4 tsp) yeast
18 g (3 tsps) salt

For the garnish
150 g (1/3 lb) sliced bacon
300 g (2/3 lb) potatoes
2 sprigs of rosemary
extra virgin olive oil
salt

METHOD

On a pastry board, mix the flour with the water and the crumbled yeast, adding the salt at the last, dissolved in a bit of water.
Let the dough rise, covered with a sheet of plastic wrap, in a warm place, until it has doubled in volume (this will take 1 to 4 hours, depending on the temperature).
Divide the dough into four pieces and form it into balls. Let it rise again, covered with plastic wrap, in a warm place, until it has doubled in volume for the second time (this will take between 30 minutes and 1 1/2 hours, depending on the temperature).
Peel and wash the potatoes, then finely slice them using an appropriate slicer or knife.
Wash, dry, and chop the rosemary.
Sprinkle the pastry board abundantly with flour, then flatten the pasta balls, starting with the tips of your fingers and continuing with a rotating movement of your hands.
Arrange the bacon and slices of potato over the pizzas, sprinkling with the chopped rosemary and a pinch of salt. Season them with a drizzle of extra virgin olive oil.
Arrange the pizzas on a baking tray and bake at 250°C (480°F) for about 8 minutes.

Preparation time: 30 Rising: 1 h 30' – 5h 30'
Cooking time: 8' Difficulty: medium

POTATO AND COTECHINO SFORMATINI

INGREDIENTS FOR **4** PEOPLE
700 g (1 1/2 lbs) potatoes
1 kg (2 1/5 lbs) cotechino (Italian sausage)
1 egg
100 g (3 1/2 oz) Parmigiano-Reggiano, grated
20 g (4 1/4 tsps) butter
salt and pepper

METHOD
Prick the cotechino sausage using a pin and then boil it, starting with cold unsalted water, for about an hour and 15 minutes. Let cool in its water, then slice.
Meanwhile, wash and boil the potatoes in their skins in lightly salted water.
After cooking, drain and peel them.
In a bowl, mash the potatoes using a potato ricer, then mix with the egg and the Parmigiano-Reggiano; season with salt and pepper.
Melt the butter, then butter the appropriate individual molds. Fill them, alternating between the potato mixture and the cotechino.
Bake at 190°C (375°F) for about 10 minutes.
Let cool for 5 minutes before removing from the molds.

Preparation time 1 h 30'
Cooking time: 10' Difficulty: easy

POTATO
AND BACON TARTLETS

INGREDIENTS FOR **4** PEOPLE

120 g (1/4 lb) puff pastry
50 g (1 3/4 oz) pancetta or thick bacon
250 g (1/2 lb) potatoes
125 ml (1/2 cup) milk
1 egg
a sprig of rosemary
salt and pepper

METHOD

Wash the potatoes and boil them with the skin on in lightly salted water.
After cooking, drain and peel them.
On a pastry board, roll out the puff pastry to a thickness of 2 mm (1/12 in).
Line four individual tartlet molds with the puff pastry.
Fill the tartlet molds with the pancetta, cut into cubes, and the potatoes,
cut into cubes or rounds.
In a bowl, whisk the egg together with the milk, salt and pepper,
and a sprig of chopped rosemary. Pour into the tartlet molds.
Bake at 180°C (350°F) for about 15 minutes.

Preparation time: 1 h
Cooking time: 15' Difficulty: easy

POTATO CAKE

INGREDIENTS FOR **4/6** PEOPLE

For the cake
325 g (2 2/3 cups) flour
120 g (1/4 lb) boiled potatoes
100 g (3 1/2 oz) pecorino cheese, grated
50 g (1 3/4 oz) pecorino cheese, in cubes
75 g butter (5 tbsps + 1 tsp) + 15 g (1 tbsp) for greasing the pan
25 g (4 tsps) yeast
80 ml (1/3 cup) water
3 eggs
50 g (1 3/4 oz) breadcrumbs
salt and freshly ground pepper

For the gratin
1 egg for browning the surface
20 g (3/4 oz) pecorino cheese, grated
freshly ground pepper

METHOD

In a large bowl, whisk the eggs with a pinch of salt, freshly ground pepper, and the cheeses. Next, stir in the melted butter and the yeast (dissolved in lukewarm water); then mix with the flour and the boiled potatoes, mashed through a potato ricer.
Fill a cake pan, previously buttered and sprinkled with breadcrumbs, halfway.
Let the dough rise until it has doubled in volume.
Brush the surface with beaten egg. Sprinkle with grated pecorino cheese and freshly ground pepper. Bake in an oven preheated to 180°C (350°F) for about 40 minutes.

Preparation time: 30' Rising: 1 h
Cooking time: 40' Difficulty: easy

POTATO
AND ANCHOVY PIE

INGREDIENTS FOR 4 PEOPLE

400 g (1 lb) potatoes
1 kg (2 1/5 lbs) fresh anchovies
100 g (3 1/2 oz) breadcrumbs
2 cherry tomatoes
1 tbsp chopped parsley
20 ml (1 tbsp + 1 tsp) extra virgin olive oil
20 g (4 1/4 tsps) butter
salt and pepper

METHOD

Clean the anchovies. Remove the heads and bones,
opening the fish book-style, then rinse.
Grease a baking pan with butter and arrange the first layer of anchovies along
its bottom in a radial pattern.
Meanwhile, peel the potatoes and slice them finely using
an appropriate instrument.
Blanch the potatoes in salted boiling water for 5 minutes.
Drain the potatoes and arrange them in layers in the baking pan,
alternating with breadcrumbs, chopped parsley, anchovies,
a drizzle of extra virgin olive oil, and a pinch of salt and pepper.
Finish with the cherry tomatoes, washed, dried, and chopped, and a drizzle of oil.
Bake at 170°C (340°F) for about 15 minutes.
Let cool for 5 minutes before removing from the baking pan.

Preparation time: 1 h
Cooking time: 15' Difficulty: medium

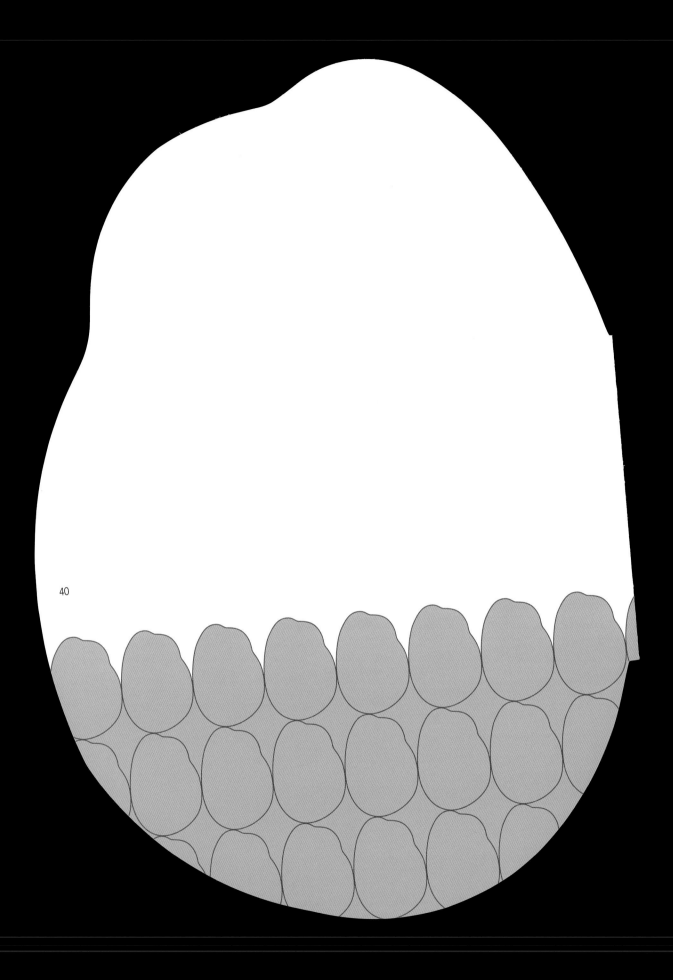

40

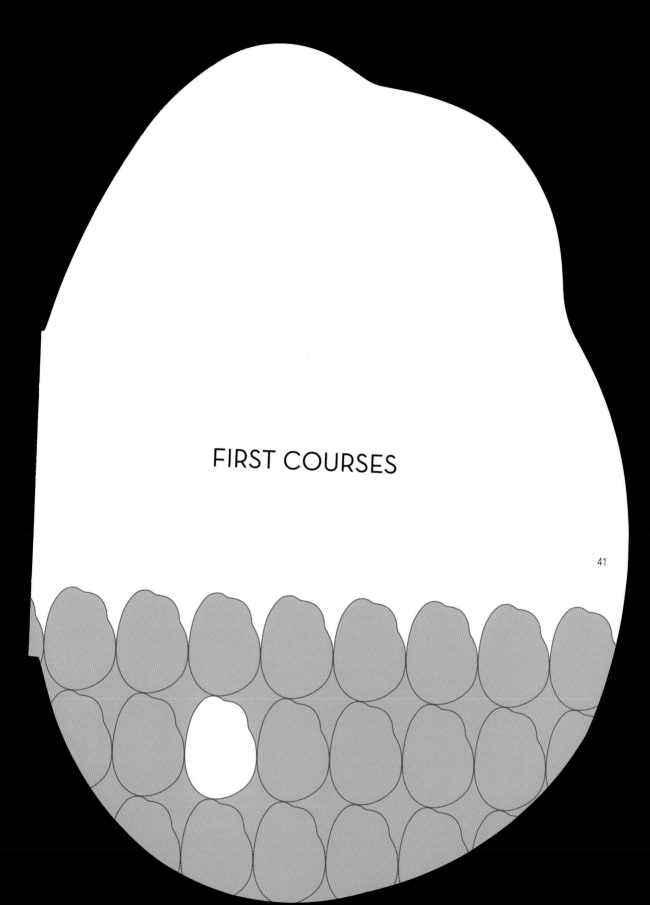

FIRST COURSES

POTATO SOUP

INGREDIENTS FOR 4/6 PEOPLE

600 g (1 1/3 lbs) potatoes
100 g (3 1/2 oz) onions
35 g (2 1/2 tbsps) butter
1.5 l (6 1/3 cups) vegetable broth or water
4/6 large croutons
salt and pepper

METHOD

Peel and wash the potatoes and cut them into cubes
(if you wish, you can cut half a potato into strips for the garnish).
Peel and finely slice the onion. Sauté it with the butter in a saucepan. Add the
potatoes and brown slightly. Add the broth or water, salt and pepper, and cook for
about 40 minutes over low heat. After cooking, make the cream by passing the
mixture through a vegetable mill or using a hand blender. When serving, if you
wish, you may add the strips of potatoes, boiled separately in salted water,
accompanied by large croutons.

Preparation time: 15'
Cooking time: 40' Difficulty: easy

POTATO GNOCCHI

INGREDIENTS FOR **4** PEOPLE

For white gnocchi
500 g (1 lbs) potatoes
70 g (1/2 cup + 1 tbsp) flour, type "00"
25 g (1 oz) Parmigiano-Reggiano,
grated
1 egg
salt

For red gnocchi
500 g (1 1/10 lbs) potatoes
60 g (2 oz) tomato concentrate

140 g (1 cups + 2 tbsp) flour, type "00"
2 eggs
salt

For green gnocchi
500 g (1 lb) potatoes
100 g (3 1/2 oz) boiled spinach
140 g (1 cup + 2 tbsp) flour, type "00"
2 eggs
salt

METHOD

Boil the potatoes, starting with cold unsalted water. After boiling, peel and mash them, using an appropriate instrument, on a pastry board. Mix the mashed potatoes with the sifted flour, egg, a pinch of salt, and, depending on the recipe, the Parmigiano-Reggiano, tomato concentrate or spinach, finely chopped. Knead the mixture using your hands, only until you obtain dough that is smooth and elastic (if necessary, depending on the type of potatoes used, you can add a bit of flour).
Divide the dough into cylinders, each about 1.5 cm (3/5 in) in diameter, then cut them into pieces about 2 cm (4/5 in) long. Boil the gnocchi in salted boiling water. Remove them using a slotted spoon as soon as they float. Season them with the sauce of your choice.

44

Preparation time: 1 h 15'
Cooking time: 4-5' Difficulty: medium

POTATO GNOCCHI
FILLED WITH TALEGGIO

INGREDIENTS FOR **4** PEOPLE

For the gnocchi
400 g (1 lb) potatoes
100 g (3/4 cup + 1 tbsp) flour, type "00"
1 egg
120 g (1/4 lb) Taleggio cheese
salt

For the sauce
40 g (1 2/5 oz) radicchio
40 g (1 2/5 oz) Prosciutto di Parma, sliced, not too thin
40 g (2 4/5 tbsps) butter

METHOD

Boil the potatoes, starting with cold unsalted water. After boiling, peel and mash them, using an appropriate instrument, on a pastry board. Mix the mashed potatoes with the sifted flour, the egg, and a pinch of salt. Using your hands, work the mixture until you obtain smooth elastic dough. Divide the dough and, on a floured pastry board, form it into cylinders about 1.5 cm (3/5 in) in diameter, then flatten to a thickness of about .5 cm (1/5 in). Place little bits of Taleggio cheese, cut into sticks about 1 cm each, centered, all down the length of the flattened gnocchi cylinders. Close the edges of the dough around the Taleggio and seal, making the strips again into cylindrical form.

Cut the strips diagonally, making gnocchi about 2 cm (4/5 in) wide. Wash the radicchio well, slice it finely, and cut the ham into thin strips.

Melt the butter in a pan and add the ham. Let it brown slightly, without letting it dry out too much, and add the radicchio, allowing it to wilt for a couple of minutes. If necessary, add a few tablespoons of water to moisten.

Boil the gnocchi in salted water. Drain them with a slotted spoon as soon as they float, and season them with the sauce.

Preparation time: 1 h 25'
Cooking time: 4-5' Difficulty: medium

PANSOTTI STUFFED
WITH POTATOES AND OLIVES

INGREDIENTS FOR 4 PEOPLE

For the dough
300 g (2 1/2 cups) white flour
3 whole eggs
1 egg white

For the filling
400 g (1 lb) potatoes
100 g (3 1/2 oz) Parmigiano-Reggiano,
grated

60 g (2 oz) black Taggiasca olives,
pitted
grated nutmeg
salt

For the seasoning
50 g (3 1/2 tbsps) butter
60 g (2 oz) Parmigiano-Reggiano, grated
thyme

METHOD

On a work surface, knead the flour with the three eggs. Let the dough, wrapped in
kitchen plastic wrap, rest in the refrigerator for 30 minutes. Boil the potatoes with
the skins on in salted water. After cooking, peel and mash them using a potato
ricer. Stir in the olives, coarsely chopped, the grated Parmigiano-Reggiano, a pinch
of salt, and a bit of freshly grated nutmeg.
Remove the dough from the refrigerator and, using a rolling pin or a special
machine, roll it out to a sheet 1 to 1 1/2 mm thick. Beat the egg white and use it to
brush the pastry. Then, cut out squares of about 6 cm (2 1/3 in) on a side and
distribute a small amount of filling (about a teaspoon) at the center of each, using
a pastry bag. Fold the squares along the diagonal, applying slight pressure on the
edges to make triangular-shaped tortelli.
In a skillet, melt the butter with the thyme.
Bring the water to a boil, add a handful of coarse salt, and immerse the pansotti.
After 3 to 4 minutes, drain them using a slotted ladle and
add them directly to the skillet to sauté with the butter and thyme.
Sprinkle with grated Parmigiano-Reggiano and serve.

Preparation time: 1 h
Cooking time: 3-4' Difficulty: medium

RICE WITH POTATOES AND LEEKS

INGREDIENTS FOR **4** PEOPLE

320 g (3/4 lb) rice
400 g (1 lb) medium potatoes
120 g (1/4 lb) leeks
30 g (2 rounded tbsps) butter
1.5 l (1 1/2 quarts) vegetable or meat broth
salt and pepper

METHOD

Peel the potatoes and cut them into cubes.
Slice the leeks and cook them in a saucepan with the butter. Add the cubed potatoes and the rice, then pour in the broth, covering the rice.
Cook, stirring frequently and adding more broth as it gradually becomes absorbed.
After cooking, season with salt and pepper.

DID YOU KNOW THAT...

The origin of the cultivation of the leek (scientific name: *Allium porrum*) is lost in the mists of time. The ancient Egyptians already knew of it and appreciated its culinary virtues. The Romans were also fond of it: Emperor Nero was given the nickname "Porrophagus" (leek eater) because he used to eat them by the dozen, not only for the flavor but also because he believed the vegetable's properties would make his voice clearer. And as we know, he was very fond of beautiful singing, accompanied by the sound of the lyre.

Preparation time: 10'
Cooking time: 20' Difficulty: easy

POTATO TORTELLI

INGREDIENTS FOR 4 PEOPLE

For the tortelli
400 g (1 lb) potatoes
150 g (1 1/4 cups) flour, type "00"
1 egg
400 g (1 lb) Taleggio cheese
salt

For the sauce
130 g (1/3 lb) cherry tomatoes
50 ml (3 1/2 tbsps) extra virgin olive oil
1 bunch chives
salt

METHOD

Boil the potatoes, starting with cold unsalted water. After boiling, peel and mash them, using an appropriate instrument, on a pastry board. Mix the purée with the sifted flour, egg, and a pinch of salt. Use your hands to work the mixture together until the dough is smooth and elastic.

On a floured pastry board, use a rolling pin to roll out the dough to a thickness of 3 to 4 mm. Cut the Taleggio into small pieces and place them on the dough, 4 to 5 cm (1 3/5 to 2 in) apart, then cover with the rest of the dough. Seal and make the tortelli, using either a knife or molds. Heat the oil in a skillet, then add the tomatoes, washed and cut into quarters. Salt them and sauté for 3 to 4 minutes. Meanwhile, boil the tortelli in salted water. As soon as they float, remove them using a slotted spoon and set them in the skillet to become flavored with the sauce. Sprinkle with finely chopped chives and serve.

Preparation time: 1 h 25'
Cooking time: 4-5' Difficulty: medium

TRENETTE
IN PESTO SAUCE WITH
POTATOES AND GREEN BEANS

INGREDIENTS FOR **4** PEOPLE
320 g (3/4 lb) trenette (pasta)
30 g (1 oz) basil
15 g (1/2 oz) pine nuts
60 g (2 oz) Parmigiano-Reggiano, grated
40 g (1 2/5 oz) seasoned pecorino, grated
1 clove garlic
200 g (2/5 lb) potatoes
100 g (1/4 lb) green beans
200 ml (3/4 cups + 1 1/2 tbsps) extra virgin olive oil (preferably Ligurian)
salt

METHOD
Hand wash the basil, then dry it in a dish towel. In a mortar, pound the basil, pine nuts, garlic, olive oil, a pinch of salt, and the grated cheeses. Alternatively, blend the ingredients in a mixer, using the pulse function to avoid overheating the pesto.
Pour it into a bowl and cover with olive oil.
In salted water, boil the potatoes, cut into cubes, and the chopped green beans. After 5 minutes, add the trenette to the same pot to cook. Drain everything and, off the heat, season with the pesto and mix well, diluting the mixture with a bit of cooking water and a drizzle of raw olive oil.

54

Preparation time: 20'
Cooking time: 12' Difficulty: easy

POTATO
AND CHESTNUT SOUP

INGREDIENTS FOR **4/6** PEOPLE

200 g (2/5 lb) dried chestnuts
250 g (1/2 lb) potatoes
50 g (1 3/4 oz) leeks
100 g (1/4 lb) onions
35 g (2 1/2 tbsps) butter
1 l (1 qt) vegetable stock
500 ml (2 cups) milk
4/6 large croutons
20 ml (1 tbsp + 1 tsp) extra virgin olive oil
salt and pepper

METHOD

Soak the dried chestnuts in cold water for 12 hours.
Then, finely chop the whites of the leeks and the onions and brown
them in a skillet with the butter.
Add the potatoes, peeled and cut into cubes, and the drained chestnuts.
Sauté briefly. Add the vegetable stock and milk, season with salt and pepper,
and cook for about an hour and 15 minutes over low heat.
After cooking, you can blend the soup or leave it more rustic.
Serve, accompanied by the large croutons and a drizzle
of raw extra virgin olive oil.

56

Preparation time: 20' Soaking: 12 h
Cooking time: 1 h 15' Difficulty: easy

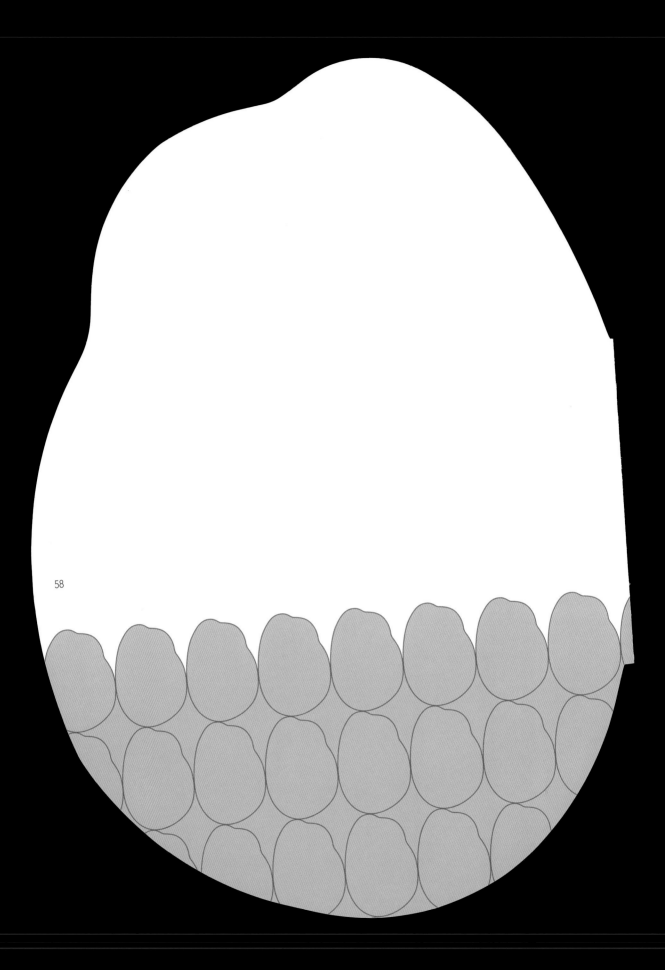
58

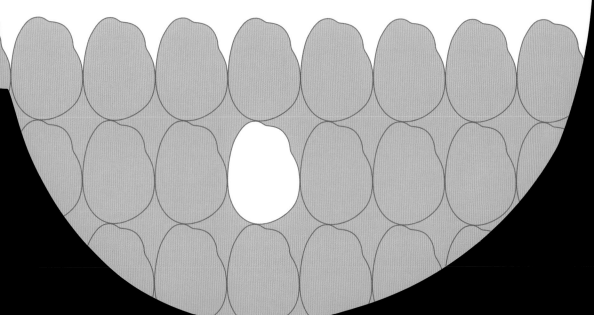

SECOND COURSES

BACCALÀ
WITH POTATOES
AND SAFFRON

INGREDIENTS FOR 4 PEOPLE
650 g (1 2/5 lbs) baccalà (dried cod)
300 g (2/3 lb) potatoes
pinch of saffron
1 tbsp chopped parsley
1 bay leaf
70 g (5 tbsps) butter
cayenne pepper
salt

METHOD
Peel the potatoes and use a small knife to give them a regular form.
Boil in a saucepan with 1 l (a little over 1 quart) salted water to which the saffron
and a bay leaf have been added; cook potatoes so that they maintain a bit of their
consistency, and keep them warm in the cooking water.
Meanwhile, cut the cod into slices, season with salt, and sauté in a skillet
with the butter, flavored with cayenne pepper as desired.
Cook for about 10 minutes, turning over halfway through cooking; toward
the end, sprinkle with chopped parsley.
Drain the potatoes, cut them into rather thick rounds, and distribute them
on the individual plates. Arrange the slices of cod over the potatoes,
garnishing to taste with cayenne pepper and parsley.

Preparation time: 40'
Cooking time: 10' Difficulty: easy

VEAL BOCCONCINI WITH POTATOES AND PEAS

INGREDIENTS FOR **4** PEOPLE

600 g (1 1/3 lbs) veal, cut into bite-size tidbits
25 g (1 oz) leek
100 g (3 1/2 oz) onion
30 g (1 oz) celery
20 g (1 2/5 tbsps) butter
1 l (1 qt) vegetable or meat stock
200 g (2/5 lb) potatoes
100 g (1/4 lb) peas
100 ml (1/3 cup + 1 1/2 tbsps) white wine
50 ml (3 1/2 tbsps) extra virgin olive oil
100 ml (1/3 cup +1 1/2 tbsps) milk
salt and pepper

METHOD

Trim and clean the leek, onion, and celery; chop them and brown them in a skillet
with the butter and oil. Add the diced veal and brown all together.
Season with salt and pepper, and drizzle with white wine.
Let the wine evaporate, and gradually moisten with the stock.
Cook for about 1 hour.
Meanwhile, peel and wash the potatoes and cut them into sticks.
Blanch for 5 minutes in salted water, drain, and mix with the morsels of meat.
Add the peas and continue cooking for about 15 minutes. Lastly, add the milk,
and reduce the sauce for a few moments.

Preparation time: 20'
Cooking time: 1 h 15' Difficulty: medium

SCALLOPS
WITH POTATOES
AND PORCINI MUSHROOMS

INGREDIENTS FOR **4** PEOPLE

4 scallops
500 g (1 lb) potatoes
350 g (3/4 lb) fresh porcini mushrooms
50 g (3 1/2 tbsps) butter
50 g (1 3/4 oz) Parmigiano-Reggiano, grated
1 egg
30 ml (2 tbsps) extra virgin olive oil
1 clove garlic
1 bunch chives
breadcrumbs
grated nutmeg
salt and pepper

METHOD

Boil the potatoes with the skins on. Drain and peel them and mash with a potato ricer. In a bowl, season the potatoes with salt and some grated nutmeg; add the butter, the grated Parmigiano-Reggiano and the egg, and mix well.
Clean the scallops and save the shells (the concave part).
Clean the porcini mushrooms, washing carefully, and slice them finely.
Set a skillet over high heat with the oil and the garlic clove, skin still on; add the mushrooms, season with salt and pepper, and sauté them, leaving them somewhat crunchy. Remove the garlic.
In another skillet, quite hot, briefly sear the scallops with a little oil. Season with salt and pepper.
Using a pastry bag with a medium-size rose tip, pipe out a ribbon of potato along the borders of the shells. Fill the prepared shells with the scallops and sautéed mushrooms. Sprinkle with breadcrumbs, drizzle with olive oil, and cook au gratin in the oven at 200°C (390°F) for 7 to 8 minutes. Garnish with the chives.

Preparation time: 1 h
Cooking time: 7-8' Difficulty: medium

SEA BASS BAKED
IN PARCHMENT WITH
POTATOES, CAPERS, AND OLIVES

INGREDIENTS FOR 4 PEOPLE

2 sea bass, filleted (500-600 g, or 1-1/3 lbs each)
200 g (2/5 lb) potatoes
80 g (2 4/5 oz) capers under salt
20 Taggiasca olives
100 ml (1/3 cup + 1 1/2 tbsps) extra virgin olive oil
1 tbsp chopped parsley
a few sprigs of rosemary
a few sage leaves
salt and pepper

METHOD

Peel and wash the potatoes and cut them into wedges. Blanch them in salted water for 5 minutes, then drain.
Season the sea bass fillets with salt and pepper and place them in baking paper packets. Over the sea bass, distribute the olives, capers (desalted in water), and potato wedges. Add a few sprigs of rosemary and a few leaves of sage, washed and dried. Drizzle with the oil and close the baking packets.
Wrap the baking paper packets individually in aluminum foil and bake at 180°C (350°F) for 12 to 15 minutes. Serve the sea bass fillets with a sprinkling of freshly chopped parsley.

Preparation time: 20'
Cooking time: 12-15' Difficulty: medium

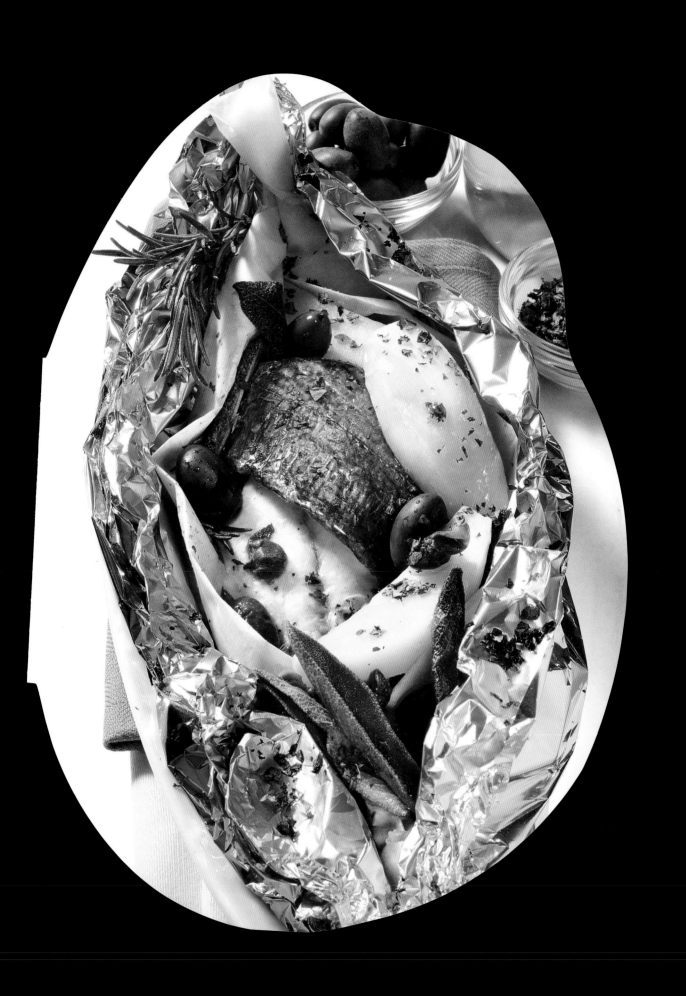

POTATO-CRUSTED SNAPPER

INGREDIENTS FOR **4** PEOPLE
1 dentex or snapper, about 1 kg (2 1/5 lbs)
350 g (3/4 lb) potatoes
40 ml (3 tbsps) extra virgin olive oil
salt and pepper

METHOD
Clean, scale, wash and fillet the snapper. Peel the potatoes; using a small knife, give them a cylindrical form and slice them, then blanch them in salted water for 1 minute.
Grease a baking pan (or line it with parchment paper), and overlap the snapper fillets; season with salt and pepper, then cover with the potato rounds, slightly overlapping one another. Drizzle with extra virgin olive oil and bake at 200°C (390°F) for 15 to 20 minutes.

DID YOU KNOW THAT...
The common dentex (scientific name: *Dentex dentex*) is a fish that has been known since ancient times, prized for its firm white paste and very delicate flavor. A lean, easily digestible fish, it lends itself well to many different forms of cooking. But it is at its best in the oven with potatoes.

Preparation time: 30'
Cooking time: 15-20' Difficulty: easy

CRUSTED FILLET
OF VEAL

INGREDIENTS FOR 4 PEOPLE
400 g (1 lb) potatoes with yellow paste
600 g (1 1/3 lbs) fillet of veal
35 ml (2 1/2 tbsps) extra virgin olive oil
fresh thyme
salt and pepper

METHOD
Peel the potatoes and cut them using a vegetable mandolin with a ripple-cut
blade, rotating them 90° between one cut and the next to produce potato "grilles."
Soak in running cold water.
Trim the veal fillet of its fat and cut it into four medallions.
Heat three-quarters of the extra virgin olive oil in a skillet with the thyme.
Remove the thyme, then sear the medallions, quickly browning them on both
sides. Season with salt and pepper.
Arrange some of the potato "grilles" on the baking sheet lined with parchment
paper. Overlap the fillets, covering with the other potatoes.
Season lightly with salt, drizzle with the remaining extra virgin olive oil,
and bake at 200°C (390°F) for 5 to 7 minutes.

Preparation time: 20'
Cooking time: 5-7' Difficulty: easy

FRITTATA WITH POTATOES, ONIONS, AND ROSEMARY

INGREDIENTS FOR **4** PEOPLE

8 eggs
400 g (1 lb) potatoes
200 g (2/5 lb) onions
2 sprigs rosemary
40 ml (3 tbsps) extra virgin olive oil
salt and pepper

METHOD

Wash the potatoes and boil them with the skins still on, until you can easily stick a fork into them. After cooking, drain, let cool, peel, and cut into cubes.
Wash and dry the rosemary; remove the leaves and chop.
Peel the onion and slice it finely; cook in a pan, with half the oil, at medium low heat for about 10 minutes, softening but not browning too much.
Season with salt and pepper.
In a bowl, beat the eggs together with salt, pepper, and rosemary.
Add the potatoes and onions. Heat the pan again with the remaining oil and when hot, pour in the egg and potato mixture. When the frittata begins to solidify, after about 5 minutes, turn it with the help of a plate and finish cooking on the other side for another 5 minutes.

Preparation time: 40'
Cooking time: 10' Difficulty: easy

POTATO TORTE

INGREDIENTS FOR 4 PEOPLE

800 g (1 3/4 lbs) potatoes
40 g (1 1/2 oz) Parmigiano-Reggiano, grated
150 g (1/3 lb) sausage, Neapolitan style
150 g (1/3 lb) cooked ham
250 g (1/2 lb) mozzarella
1 tbsp chopped parsley
2 eggs
20 g (1 2/5 tbsps) butter
50 g (1 3/4 oz) breadcrumbs
salt and pepper

METHOD

Wash the potatoes and boil them with the skins on. Drain, let cool, and peel. Mash them using a potato ricer and put them into a bowl. Add the eggs, the grated Parmigiano-Reggiano, and the sausage, ham, and mozzarella, cut into cubes. Season with a pinch of salt and a sprinkling of pepper; add the chopped parsley. Butter a single mold or four individual molds; dust with breadcrumbs and fill with the mixture. Level the surface and top with breadcrumbs and a few shavings of butter. (Rather than mixing the various ingredients together, you can arrange them in alternating layers: first the potato mixture, then the ham, sausage, and lastly the mozzarella, ending with a layer of potatoes.)
Bake the gattò for about 30 minutes at about 170°C (340°F).

74

Preparation time: 1 h
Cooking time: 30' Difficulty: easy

CHICKEN
AND POTATO SALAD

INGREDIENTS FOR **4/6** PEOPLE

150 g (1/3 lb) boiled potatoes
400 g (1 lb) chicken breasts
200 g (2/5 lb) mixed salad leaves
150 ml (2/3 cup) balsamic vinegar
50 ml (3 1/2 tbsps) extra virgin olive oil
a few sage leaves
sprig of rosemary
salt and pepper

METHOD

Trim and wash the mixed salad leaves. Wash the rosemary and sage,
and chop half of it. Separate and clean the chicken breasts.
In a skillet over medium heat, put the balsamic vinegar (keep aside 3 tablespoons
for the sauce), salt, the chopped herbs, and the chicken breasts.
Cover with water and bring to a boil.
After cooking, remove the breasts from the liquid and let them cool.
Cut the chicken into strips and season with a little extra virgin olive oil,
the chopped herbs and a sprinkling of freshly ground pepper.
On the plates, arrange some of the salad, seasoned with the remaining oil
and balsamic vinegar, and emulsified along with a pinch of salt. On top of this,
arrange the slices of chicken and the potatoes cut into wedges.

76

Preparation time: 15' Cooking time: 20'
Cooling: 30' Difficulty: easy

POTATO
AND VEAL MEATBALLS

INGREDIENTS FOR 4 PEOPLE
200 g (2/5 lb) veal
250 g (1/2 lb) boiled potatoes
1 egg
100 g (3 1/2 oz) Parmigiano-Reggiano, grated
nutmeg
oil for frying
salt and pepper

METHOD
Peel the boiled potatoes and mash them in a bowl using a potato ricer. Chop the meat and mix it with the potatoes. Season with salt and pepper and a bit of freshly grated nutmeg. Add the grated Parmigiano-Reggiano and the egg.
Form the meatballs, flatten them slightly, and fry in the oil, not too hot, to allow an even cooking on the inside. Drain and set to dry on paper towels.

DID YOU KNOW THAT...
Nutmeg, which is the seed of the *Myristica fragrans*, is frequently used as a spice in Italian cooking, especially in fillings made with meat and cheese. Its aroma, warm and spicy, exotic and fascinating, gives dishes an intense and special flavor. It should, however, be used sparingly: if ingested in high doses (over 10 g), it can result in altered states of consciousness, possibly with visual hallucinations.

Preparation time: 20'
Cooking time: 7-8' Difficulty: easy

OCTOPUS
WITH POTATOES

INGREDIENTS FOR **4** PEOPLE

500 g (1 lb) octopus
500 g (1 lb) potatoes
1 onion
1 carrot
3 stalks of celery
80 g (2 4/5 oz) black olives
100 ml (1/3 cup + 1 1/2 tbsps) extra virgin olive oil
1 lemon
1 tbsp chopped parsley
salt and pepper

METHOD

Place a pot of salted water on the burner; when it comes to a boil, add the onion,
carrot, and one stalk of celery, previously trimmed and washed.
Cook for 5 minutes, then place the octopus in the water, making sure to dip it
three times in the hot water before leaving to cook to make it more tender.
Cook it for an hour or until it is soft; test by piercing with a knife.
After cooking, turn off the heat, cover the pot, and let cool for an hour.
In the meanwhile, peel and wash the potatoes and cook them in boiling salted
water for 15 to 20 minutes, or until a wooden skewer easily penetrates them.
Drain, let cool, and cut them, as desired, into wedges or cubes.
Also cut the remaining celery, trimmed and washed, into pieces.
Squeeze the lemon; in a bowl, emulsify the lemon with the oil, salt,
and pepper. After the octopus has cooled, drain and cut it into pieces.
Then prepare the salad by mixing the potatoes, celery, black olives, and octopus.
Season with the sauce you previously prepared and with a sprinkling
of chopped parsley.
Drizzle with the remaining extra virgin olive oil and serve.

Preparation time: 15' Cooking time: 1 h
Cooling: 1 h Difficulty: easy

SALMON
WITH POTATOES AND EGGS

INGREDIENTS FOR 4 PEOPLE

600 g (1 1/3 lbs) salmon fillets
400 g (1 lb) potatoes
2 eggs
1 tbsp chopped parsley
50 g (3 1/2 tbsps) butter
salt and pepper

METHOD

Boil the eggs for about 10 minutes. Cool them under cold water.
Peel the potatoes and make little potato balls using a special corer with
a diameter of 2.5 cm (1 in).
Blanch the potato balls in salted water for 5 minutes.
Divide the salmon fillet into four slices; season with salt and pepper.
Melt the butter in a saucepan and when it begins to foam, brown the salmon
on both sides. Add the potatoes and bake in the oven at 180°C (350°F)
for 7 to 8 minutes.
After removing from the oven, sprinkle with parsley and serve on plates.
Sprinkle the servings with sieved hard-boiled eggs.

Preparation time: 30'
Cooking time: 7-8' Difficulty: easy

OVEN-BAKED RICE, POTATOES, AND MUSSELS

INGREDIENTS FOR **4** PEOPLE
250 g (3/5 lb) Ribe rice
80 g (2 4/5) pecorino cheese, grated
600 g (1 1/3 lbs) mussels
350 g (12 oz) cherry tomatoes
300 g (10 1/2 oz) potatoes
180 g (6.3 oz) onions
100 ml (1/3 cup + 1 1/2 tbsps) extra virgin olive oil
500-600 ml (2 to 2 1/2 cups) water
1 clove garlic
2 tbsps chopped parsley
salt and pepper

METHOD
Clean the mussels thoroughly, scraping under running water, then open them using a small knife. This operation should be performed over a container to collect the liquid, which will later be used in the cooking. Discard any empty shells.
Peel and slice the potatoes and onions. Mince the garlic.
Cut half the cherry tomatoes into wedges, and leave the rest whole.
Drizzle a bit of extra virgin olive oil over the bottom of a baking dish of suitable size. Inside, arrange a layer of onions and distribute half the garlic, parsley, and cherry tomatoes. Season with salt and pepper, sprinkle the grated pecorino cheese over the top, and finish with half the sliced potatoes.
Cover with all the rice, rinsed and drained, then arrange the mussels over the top. Make another layer with the rest of the garlic and parsley, cherry tomatoes, and remaining potatoes. Season again with salt and pepper. Sprinkle with the remaining grated pecorino cheese, and drizzle with plenty of olive oil.
Lastly, cover with the liquid saved from the mussels, adding additional water to completely cover the ingredients.
Bake the casserole (referred to in Italian as a *tiella*) at 180°C (350°F) for about 45 minutes, or until the rice is cooked to perfection.

Preparation time: 30'
Cooking time: 30' Difficulty: easy

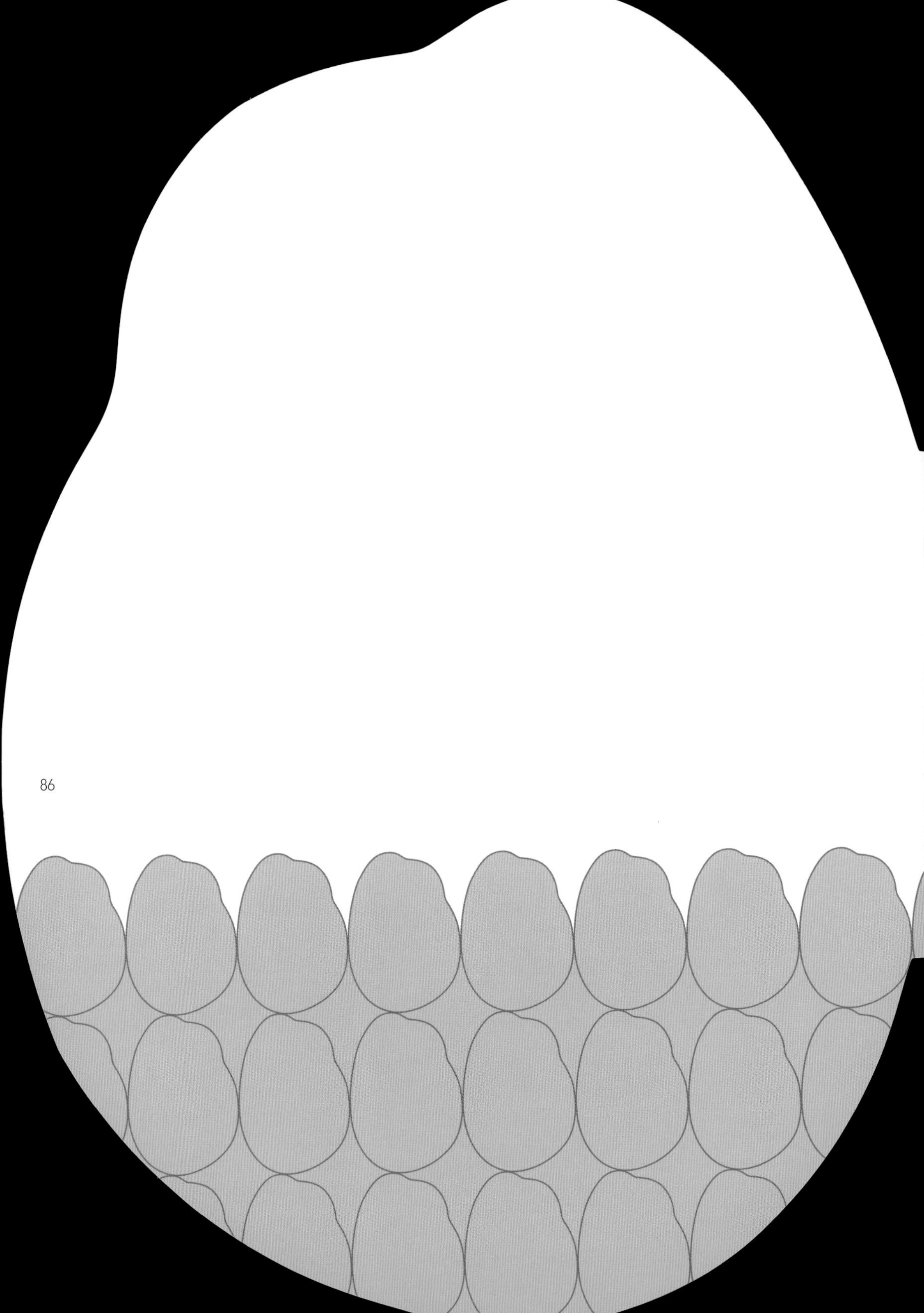

SIDE DISHES

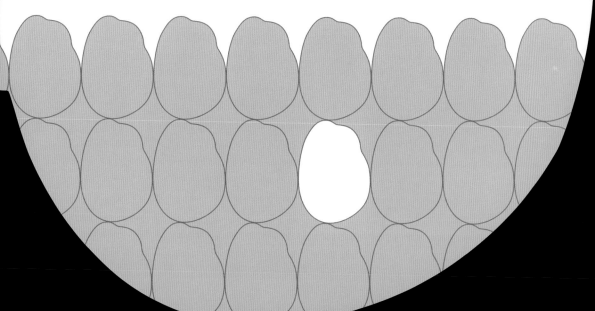

POTATO BASKETS WITH PURPLE POTATO CHIPS

INGREDIENTS FOR **4** PEOPLE

400 g (1 lb) potatoes with yellow paste
200 g (1/2 lb) potatoes with purple paste
oil for frying
salt

METHOD

Peel the potatoes.
Cut the purple potatoes into thin rounds using a special mandolin,
and put them under cold running water.
Next, cut the yellow potatoes with a mandolin, using the ripple-cut blade
and rotating the potato by 90° between one cut and the next, so as to obtain
crossed- grille designs on the potato rounds. Set these, as well,
to soak in cold running water.
Arrange some potato "grilles" along the bottom of a special two-part round
fry basket; close the fry basket.
Immerse the device in boiling oil until the potato baskets have turned golden.
Drain and let dry on paper towels. Salt lightly. Repeat until all the potato "grille"
rounds have been used.
When the potato baskets are ready, fry the purple potato chips. Drain them with
a slotted spoon, set them on parchment paper, and season with salt.
Fill the potato baskets with the purple potato chips and serve.

Preparation time: 30'
Cooking time: 3-5' Difficulty: easy

POTATO CROQUETTES WITH BACON, GORGONZOLA, AND ALMONDS

INGREDIENTS FOR **4** PEOPLE
130 g (4 1/2 oz) speck, or thick bacon
500 g (1 lb) potatoes
100 g (3 1/2 oz) Gorgonzola
15 g (1/2 oz) slivered almonds
2 eggs
oil for frying
salt and pepper

METHOD
Wash the potatoes and boil them in lightly salted water. After cooking,
mash them into a bowl using a potato ricer.
Meanwhile, cut the bacon or speck into small cubes, and cut the Gorgonzola into
little pieces. Mix these together with the mashed potatoes and the eggs,
and correct for salt and pepper.
Shape the mixture into balls about the size of eggs; you can form them
into cylinders or patties, then roll them in the slivered almonds.
Fry the croquettes in abundant hot oil, then drain them and set to dry
on paper towels. Season with salt.

DID YOU KNOW THAT...
Gorgonzola, one of the best known and appreciated Italian cheeses in the world,
owes its name to the town near Milan where it was born.
According to legend, it was invented there, around the 12th century.
A cheese maker by the name of Piermarco Bergamo happened to work together
the curd from the previous evening with that of the morning, thus obtaining
a product in which mold formed.

Preparation time: 40'
Cooking time: 5' Difficulty: medium

POTATO
SALAD

INGREDIENTS FOR **4/6** PEOPLE

600 g (1 1/3 lbs) potatoes, boiled with the skins on
(with yellow, white, and purple paste)
100 ml (1/3 cup + 1 1/2 tbsps) plain yogurt
100 ml (1/3 cup + 1 1/2 tbsps) extra virgin olive oil
chives
salt

METHOD

Peel the boiled potatoes and cut them into cubes about 2 cm (4/5 in)
per side; place them in a bowl.
Prepare the sauce by mixing the yogurt with the extra virgin olive oil
and a pinch of salt.
Season the potatoes with the sauce. Arrange the salad on a serving plate,
decorating it with strands of fresh chives.

DID YOU KNOW THAT...

Chives (scientific name: Allium schoenoprasum) are used almost exclusively
in recipes that are served cool, because their aroma is so delicate that it
risks becoming lost in cooking. Usually, chives are taken directly from the
plant at the time of use; after a quick rinse, they are minced with scissors.
Due to their elasticity, they are also used to hold together small preparations,
such as little bunches of boiled asparagus or small rolls of bresaola filled
with soft goat cheese.

Preparation time: 20'
Difficulty: easy

POTATO MILLE-FEUILLE

INGREDIENTS FOR **4/6** PEOPLE

600 g (1 1/3 lbs) potatoes, with yellow, white, and purple paste
50 ml (3 1/2 tablespoons) extra virgin olive oil
200 g (2/5 lb) tomatoes
a few sprigs of thyme
salt, pepper

METHOD

Wash the potatoes and boil them for 12 to 15 minutes (they should remain rather firm).
Let cool, then peel them and cut them into slices about 5 to 6 mm (1/4 in) thick.
Finish cooking the slices for a few minutes on a very hot grill (or griddle) greased with oil.
Season with salt, pepper, a drizzle of extra virgin olive oil, and a few sprigs of thyme.
Assemble the mille-feuille by layering potato slices in a baking pan.
Wash and dry the tomatoes, removing their seeds, and chop them into cubes.
Garnish the mille-feuille with the tomatoes.

DID YOU KNOW THAT...

Thyme (scientific name: *Thymus*) derives its name from the Greek term thymos, meaning "soul, vital principle." Owing to its pleasant and aromatic perfume, it was thought since ancient times to be capable of awakening strength and courage in those who sniffed it. It may perhaps not be capable of giving vigor and courage, but certainly its numerous medicinal properties have been known for thousands of years.

Preparation time: 30'
Difficulty: easy

BAKED POTATOES
WITH TOMATOES
AND ONIONS

INGREDIENTS FOR 4 PEOPLE

600 g (1 1/3 lbs) potatoes
300 g (2/3 lb) yellow onions
400 g (1 lb) tomatoes
40 ml (3 tbsps) extra virgin olive oil
40 g (1 2/5 oz) pecorino cheese, grated
salt and pepper

METHOD

Wash and peel the potatoes. Cut them into rounds 3 to 4 mm (1/8 in) thick
and keep them in cold water.
Wash the tomatoes and slice them into rounds about 5 mm (1/5 in) thick.
Peel the onions and cut them into rings 2 to 3 mm (1/10 in) thick.
Cover a baking pan with parchment paper and arrange the potatoes, tomatoes,
and onions on it, alternating them until all the ingredients have been used.
Season with salt and pepper.
Finish with a drizzle of olive oil and a sprinkling of grated pecorino cheese.
Bake at 180°C (350°F) for about 20 minutes. Cover with a sheet of aluminum foil
if the vegetables become too dry.

DID YOU KNOW THAT...

Potatoes, like other Solanaceae, contain several toxins, particularly an alkaloid
called solanine, so they should never be cooked when they have parts that
are green or have started sprouting. It is best to store them in the dark
and eat them without the skins, because it is there that the majority
of the solanine, is concentrated and is not eliminated with cooking.

Preparation time: 20'
Cooking time: 20' Difficulty: easy

FRIED
POTATOES

INGREDIENTS FOR 4 PEOPLE
400 g (1 lb) potatoes with yellow paste
oil for frying
salt

METHOD
Peel the potatoes and set them into a bowl with cold water.
For "Paris-style" potatoes, make little balls using a special corer with a diameter
of 2.5 cm (1 in).
For "hazelnut-style" potatoes, make little balls using a special corer
with a diameter of 2 cm (4/5 in).
For "chips," cut the potatoes into very thin slices using a special mandolin.
For "French fried" potatoes, cut them into regular slices of about 7 mm (1/4 in),
then into sticks of the same size.
For "grille" potatoes, cut them using a ripple-cut blade, rotating the potato
by 90° between one cut and the next.
For "matchstick" potatoes, cut them into regular slices of about 2 mm (1/10 in),
then into sticks of the same size.
For "Newbridge" potatoes, cut them into regular slices of about 12 mm (1/2 in),
then into sticks of the same size.
Immerse the potatoes in cold water and rinse them several times.
Fry each cut separately. For each of the cuts (except the chips, grilles,
and matchsticks): drain the potatoes and dry them. Fry them in abundant oil
at 150°C (300°F) for about 5 minutes or until cooked, but not until darkened.
Drain them, then increase the temperature of the oil to 180°C (350°F).
Immerse the partially cooked potatoes again, for the time necessary to obtain
the classic golden crust. Drain them on paper towels and season with salt.
For the chips, grilles, and matchsticks, there is no need for precooking
at 150°C (300°F): proceed directly to frying at 180°C (350°F).

Preparation time: 20'
Cooking time: 5-7' Difficulty: easy

POTATOES STUFFED WITH CAPRINO (GOAT CHEESE)

INGREDIENTS FOR 4 PEOPLE

4 medium potatoes
150 g (1/3 lb) fresh caprino (goat cheese)
salt and pepper

METHOD

Wash the potatoes, leaving their skins on. Wrap them individually
in aluminum foil and bake in the oven at 180°C (350°F) for about 30 minutes.
After cooking, cut them in half, season with a pinch of salt,
and top each potato half with a tablespoon of fresh caprino
and a sprinkling of freshly ground pepper.

DID YOU KNOW THAT...

The "caprini" or goat cheeses – whether fresh and creamy with
a soft consistency or seasoned and with a semi-hard consistency – represent
a dairy highlight of many Italian regions, from Sicily to Trentino-Alto Adige.
Fresh caprini have an odor of sour milk and yogurt, with a slightly acidic flavor,
not salty. They can be eaten alone, flavored with herbs or spices,
with a drizzle of olive oil and a pinch of salt, with fresh vegetables,
marinated in oil, or even with honey. You can also use them to stuff baked
vegetables or as ingredients in pasta sauces.

Preparation time: 10'
Cooking time: 30' Difficulty: easy

POTATO POLENTA

INGREDIENTS FOR **4/6** PEOPLE

250 g (1 1/2 cups) polenta meal
500 g (1 lb) potatoes
35 g (2 1/2 tablespoons) butter
1.5 l (6 1/3 cups) water
salt

METHOD

Peel the potatoes, wash them and cut into cubes.
In a saucepan, bring the water to a boil with the butter,
add salt and cook the potatoes. After about 15 minutes, pour in the polenta meal,
mixing with a whisk. Cook over low heat, stirring with a wooden spoon
for about 40 minutes. Serve immediately, garnished as desired with cheeses.
Any leftover polenta can be cut into slices and reheated in the oven,
on the grill, or in the frying pan.

DID YOU KNOW THAT...

The ancient dish of polenta is based on flour from grains, water and salt.
Part of the Italian tradition, it is used especially in cuisines of the northern region,
such as Lombardy, the Veneto, Trentino, Emilia-Romagna, and Friuli-Venezia Giulia.
Potato polenta is typical of southern Trentino, where it is often flavored with
other ingredients added at the end of the cooking process,
such as pieces of local salami, bits of cheese, fried onions ...

Preparation time: 15'
Cooking time: 1 h Difficulty: easy

MASHED POTATOES

INGREDIENTS FOR **4/6** PEOPLE

Classic
500 g (1 lb) potatoes
350 ml (1 1/2 cups) milk
80 g (5 1/2 tbsps) butter
100 g (3 1/2 oz) Parmigiano-Reggiano,
grated
nutmeg
salt

With carrots
250 g (1/2 lb) potatoes
500 g (1 lb) carrots
180 ml (3/4 cup) milk
30 g (2 rounded tbsps) butter

70 g (2 1/2 oz) Parmigiano-Reggiano,
grated
nutmeg
salt

With peas
200 g (2/5 lb) potatoes
500 g (1 lb) peas
150 ml (6 1/3 cups) milk
30 g (2 rounded tbsps) butter
50 g (1 3/4 oz) Parmigiano-Reggiano,
grated
nutmeg
salt

METHOD

Peel the potatoes and boil them in lightly salted water for about 25 minutes
(make sure they are completely cooked by sticking a small knife into one).
For the flavored mashed potatoes, cooked the other vegetables together
with the potatoes.
Pass the vegetables through a food mill or a potato ricer and
put them in a pan. Combine the butter, the grated Parmigiano-Reggiano cheese,
and some freshly grated nutmeg.
In a separate pan, heat the milk to just below boiling and add to the
mashed potatoes. Season with salt, mix thoroughly, and serve.

Preparation time: 20'
Difficulty: easy

RÖSTI

INGREDIENTS FOR 4/6 PEOPLE
750 g (1 3/4 lbs) potatoes
50 g (3 1/2 tbsps) butter
salt and pepper

METHOD
Peel the potatoes, then wash and grate them.
Melt the butter in a skillet, preferably nonstick, and add the potatoes.
Add salt and pepper, and stir using two spatulas.
When the potatoes begin to soften, flatten them using the spatulas,
shaping them into the form of a pancake. Let them form a golden crust,
then turn them over as a whole, like a frittata, and brown the other side.

DID YOU KNOW THAT...
Rösti is a traditional dish of Switzerland. It is served as a side dish or a main dish.
The basic recipe, which uses only potatoes (raw or previously boiled),
butter, and a pinch of salt and pepper, has many variants throughout
the various Swiss cantons.
It can be enriched with onions, bacon, eggs, cheese, herbs, apples ...

Preparation time: 10'
Cooking time: 15' Difficulty: easy

POTATOES
AU GRATIN

INGREDIENTS FOR **4** PEOPLE

400 g (1 lb) potatoes
200 ml (3/4 cup + 1 1/2 tbsps) fresh cream
150 ml (2/3 cup) milk
10 g (3/4 tbsp) butter for greasing the pan
1 clove garlic
fine salt
white pepper

METHOD

Peel and wash the potatoes. Cut the potatoes into very thin slices using a
vegetable mandolin or slicer. Pour the cream into a saucepan and add the milk,
potatoes, salt, pepper, and the clove of garlic, whole.
Place the saucepan over moderate heat, cover with a lid,
and cook until the potatoes are soft. Remove the garlic.
Butter a baking dish and arrange the potatoes along the bottom.
Bake at 180°C (350°F) for about 20 minutes, until the surface of the potatoes
has begun to brown. In order to obtain a regular cut, allow the potatoes
to cool before cutting into shapes as desired.
Before serving, reheat in the oven at 180°C (350°F) for several minutes.

Preparation time: 20'
Cooking time: 35-40' Difficulty: easy

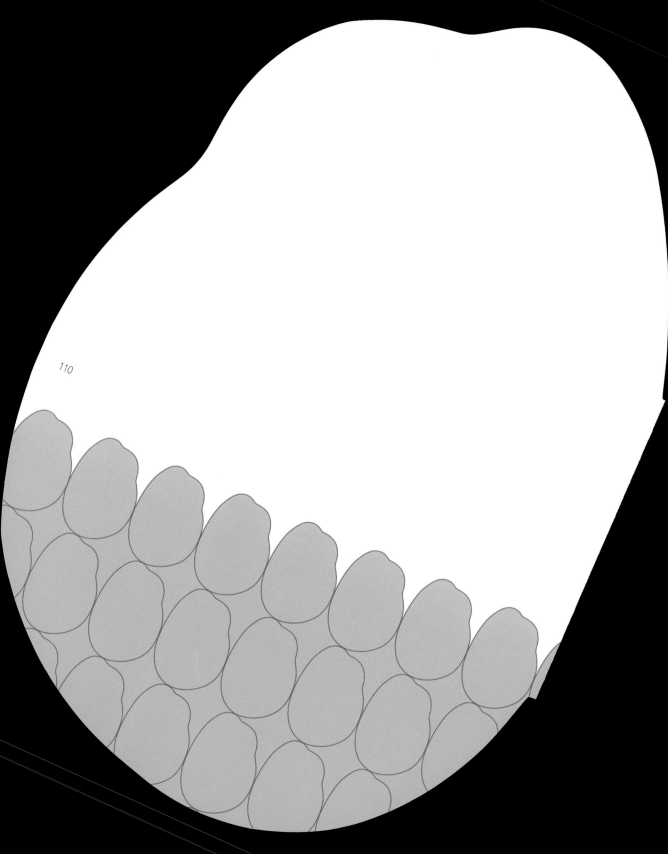

DESSERTS

111

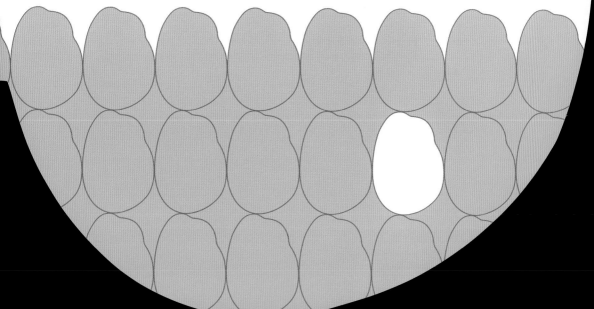

POTATO
DOUGHNUTS

INGREDIENTS FOR 4 PEOPLE
500 g (3 4/5 cups) flour
250 g (1/2 lb) potatoes
10 g (1 1/2 tsps) yeast
10 g (1 1/2 tsps) sugar
50 g (3 1/2 tbsps) butter
pinch of salt
2 eggs
100 ml (1/3 cup + 1 1/2 tbsps) milk
oil for frying
sugar for decoration

METHOD
Wash and boil the potatoes with the skins on. After cooking, mash them with
a potato ricer and let them cool. Mix the flour with the mashed potatoes,
the yeast dissolved in part of the milk, the eggs, and the sugar.
Mix with the remaining milk. Lastly, mix in the butter, softened to room
temperature, and a pinch of salt. Knead until you obtain smooth, elastic dough.
Cover the dough and let it rise for about 30 minutes at room temperature.
Then, on a floured pastry board, roll it out with a rolling pin to a thickness
of about 2 cm (4/5 in), and cut into discs of about 10 cm (4 in) diameter
using a pastry ring.
Place the dough rounds onto a tray covered with a floured towel.
Let them rise until doubled in volume (this will take at least an hour).
Fry the doughnuts in abundant boiling oil until they are golden in color.
Drain and set to dry on absorbent paper, then pass them through the sugar.

Preparation time: 40' Rising: 1 h 30'
Cooking time: 5' Difficulty: medium

SWEET POTATO PUDDING

INGREDIENTS FOR 4 PEOPLE

250 g (1/2 lb) sweet potatoes
40 g (2 4/5 tbsps) butter
100 ml (1/3 cup + 1 1/2 tbsps) cream
20 g (1/2 tbsp) flour
40 g (3 tbsps) sugar
1 egg
40 g (1 2/5 oz) pine nuts
50 g (1 3/4 oz) raisins
pinch of cinnamon
10 g (3/4 tbsp) butter for greasing

METHOD

Wash and boil the potatoes with the skins on. Peel and let cool, then mash them using a potato ricer. Place them in a saucepan with the butter, cream, and flour. Stir and cook for 2 minutes. Remove from the heat and add the sugar, pine nuts, and raisins (softened previously in water for 10 minutes, then squeezed dry), the cinnamon, and the egg yolk.
Whip the egg white until fluffy and gently incorporate into the mixture, using a spatula and stirring from bottom to top.
Grease the individual molds with butter, and fill the molds three-quarters full with the mixture. Bake in a bain-marie at 180°C (350°F) for about 35 minutes. Let the puddings cool before removing them from the molds. If you like, sprinkle with cocoa powder.

Preparation time: 20'
Cooking time: 35' Difficulty: medium

POTATO
SORBET

INGREDIENTS FOR **4/6** PEOPLE

500 g (1 lb) boiled potatoes (with yellow, white, or purple paste)
500 ml (2 cups) water
60 g (2 oz) dextrose
250 g (1/2 lb) sugar
10 g (1 1/2 tsps) stabilizer

METHOD

Pass the boiled potatoes through a potato ricer. The color and aroma of the
sorbet will depend upon the type of potato used.
In a bowl, mix the sugar with the dextrose and stabilizer. In a pan, heat the water
to 65°C (150°F) and pour it into the sugar mixture as a shower, carefully mixing
it in with a whisk. Mix in the potatoes as well and quickly let the mixture cool
to 4°C (40°F), by placing it in a bowl immersed in a basin of water and ice.
Leave it to mature at 4°C (40°F) for six hours, then freeze, stirring in an ice cream
maker until the mixture becomes foamy and dry in appearance, that is, not shiny
(the time required will depend upon the ice cream maker used).

Preparation time: 20'
Maturation: 6 h Difficulty: easy

STRUDEL
WITH SWEET POTATOES, APPLES, AND WALNUTS

INGREDIENTS FOR 4 PEOPLE

For the dough
250 g (scant 2 cups) flour
1 egg
80 ml (1/3 cup) water
20 ml (1 tbsp + 1 tsp) extra virgin olive oil
pinch of salt

For the filling
250 g (1/2 lb) boiled sweet potatoes
250 g (1/2 lb) apples

100 g (3 1/2 oz) walnuts
50 g (1 3/4 oz) prima raisins
50 g (3 1/2 tbsps) butter
breadcrumbs (if necessary)
cinnamon

For the finishing
1 egg
powdered sugar

METHOD

On a pastry board, prepare the dough, kneading together all the ingredients.
Form the dough into a ball and let it rest for at least 30 minutes,
covered with kitchen plastic wrap.
Meanwhile, cut the sweet potatoes into slices; peel the apples and cut these into
slices also. Sauté these in a pan with the butter, then add the raisins (softened
previously in warm water for 15 minutes, then squeezed dry), the walnuts,
chopped, and a pinch of cinnamon.
Adjust the consistency of the filling, if necessary, with a few breadcrumbs.
Roll out the dough into a thin sheet, widening it on the backs of your fists.
Arrange the filling along the long side of the dough, and roll it over on itself.
Coat the surface of the strudel with beaten egg and bake in the oven at 170°C
to 180°C (340°F to 360°F) for 15 to 20 minutes.
A few minutes before the strudel is done, sprinkle it with powdered sugar,
then allow it to finish baking.

118

Preparation time: 1 h
Cooking time: 15-20' Difficulty: medium

SWEET POTATO PIE

INGREDIENTS FOR 4 PEOPLE

For the crust
250 g (1/2 lb) dried cookies
80 g (5 3/5 tbsps) butter
60 g (2 oz) cocoa powder
40 g (1 2/5 oz) sugar

For the filling
500 g (1 1/10 lbs) sweet potatoes
120 g (1/2 cup + 1 1/2 tbsps) sugar
2 eggs
1 tbsp liqueur of your choice
1/2 lemon
pinch of cinnamon
10 g (3/4 tbsp) butter for greasing
powdered sugar
slivered almonds

METHOD

To prepare the pie crust, crumble the cookies and mix them together
with the melted butter, cocoa powder, and sugar.
Spread out this base in a buttered pie pan and allow
it to cool for 30 minutes in the refrigerator.
Boil the sweet potatoes with the skins on. Peel and let cool, then mash with
a potato ricer. Mix them together in a bowl with the sugar, eggs, liqueur, lemon
juice, and cinnamon. Pour the filling into a pie pan and bake at 180°C (350°F)
for 20 to 25 minutes.
Let the pie cool before serving. If you like, sprinkle with powdered sugar
and/or slivered almonds.

Preparation time: 1 h
Cooking time: 25' Difficulty: medium

ALPHABETICAL
INDEX OF RECIPES

ALPHABETICAL
INDEX OF INGREDIENTS

125

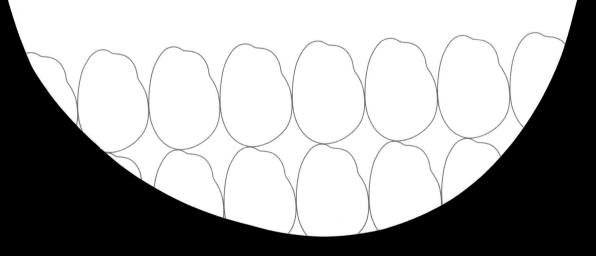

ACADEMIA BARILLA

AMBASSADOR OF ITALIAN
GASTRONOMY THROUGHOUT THE WORLD

In the heart of Parma, one of the most distinguished capitals of Italian cuisine, is the Barilla Center. Set in the grounds of the former Barilla pasta factory, this modern architectural complex is the home of Academia Barilla. This was founded in 2004 to promote the art of Italian cuisine, protecting the regional gastronomic heritage and safeguarding it from imitations and counterfeits, while encouraging the great traditions of the Italian restaurant industry. Academia Barilla is also a center of great professionalism and talent that is exceptional in the world of cooking. It organizes cooking classes for culinary enthusiasts, it provides services for those involved in the restaurant industry, and it offers products of the highest quality. In 2007, Academia Barilla was awarded the "Premio Impresa-Cultura" for its campaigns promoting the culture and creativity of Italian gastronomy throughout the world. The center was designed to meet the training requirements of the world of food and it is equipped with all the multimedia facilities necessary for organizing major events. The remarkable gastronomic auditorium is surrounded by a restaurant, a laboratory for sensory analysis, and various teaching rooms equipped with the most modern technology. The Gastronomic Library contains over 10,000 books and a remarkable collection of historic menus as well as prints related to culinary subjects. The vast cultural heritage of the library can be consulted on the internet which provides access to hundreds of digitized historic texts. This avant-garde approach and the presence of a team of internationally famous experts enables Academia Barilla to offer a wide range of courses, meeting the needs of both restaurant chefs and amateur food lovers. In addition, Academia Barilla arranges cultural events and activities aiming to develop the art of cooking, supervised by experts, chefs, and food critics, that are open to the public. It also organizes the "Academia Barilla Film Award", for short films devoted to Italy's culinary traditions.

www.academiabarilla.com

WS White Star Publishers® is a registered trademark
property of of De Agostini Libri S.p.A.

© 2012 De Agostini Libri S.p.A.
Via G. da Verrazano, 15
28100 Novara, Italy
www.whitestar.it - www.deagostini.it

Translation: John Venerella
Editing: Suzanne Smither

ISBN 978-88-544-0670-4
3 4 5 6   17 16 15 14 13

Printed in China

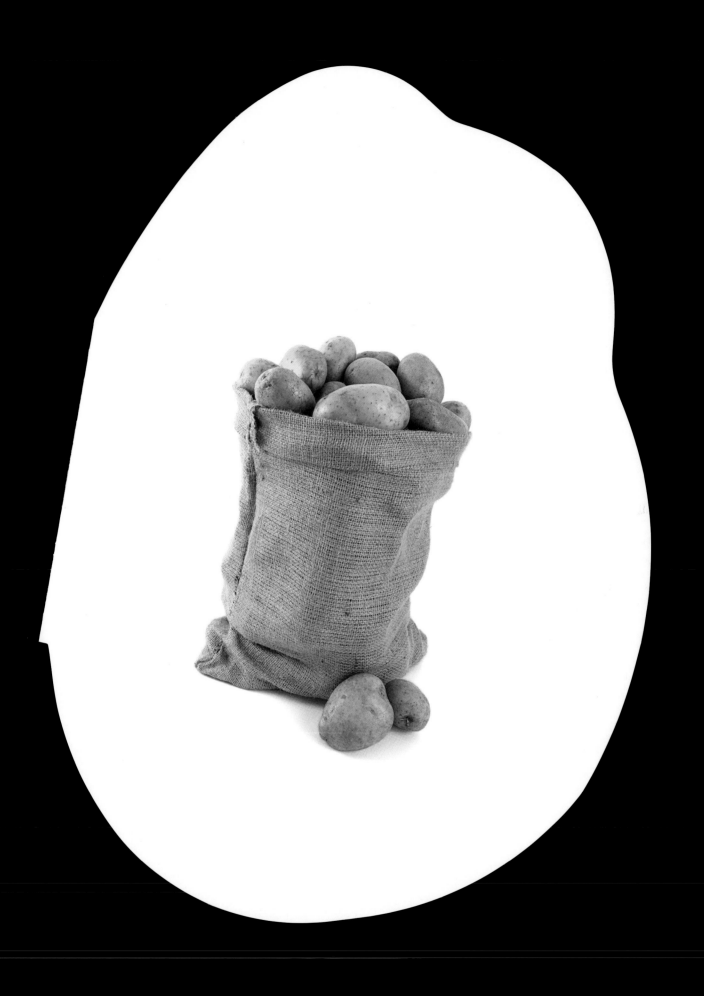

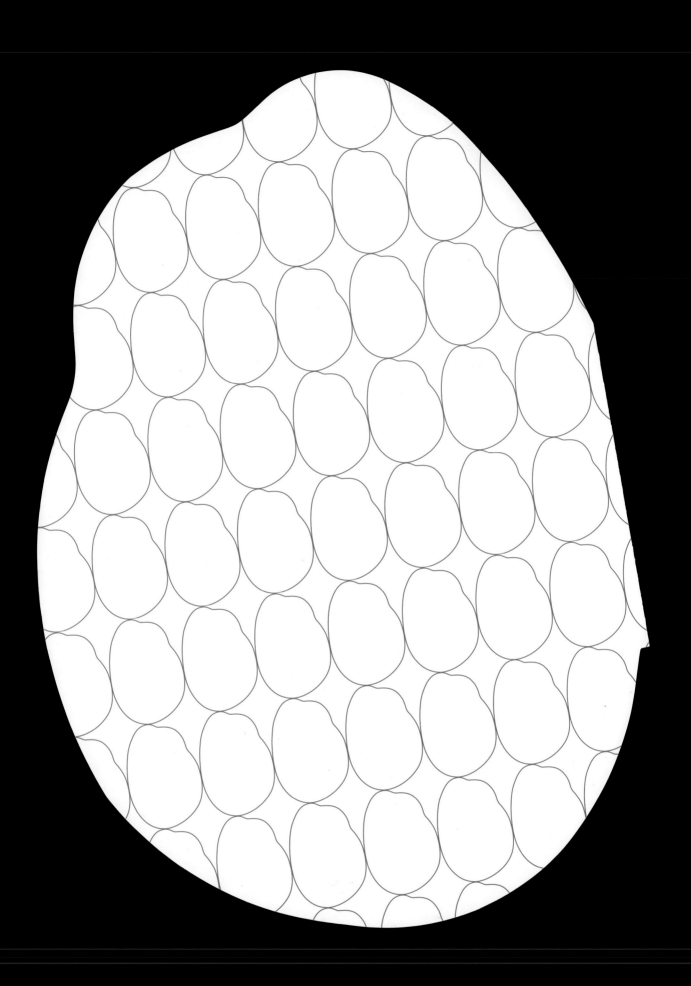